'Down-to-earth and informative, this book provides practical information for busy professionals who come into contact with children who have eating disorders. Creative analogies demystify the eating disorders and case illustrations paint a vivid picture of how to help. I highly recommend this valuable resource.'

— *Josie Geller, Director of Research, Eating Disorders Program, St. Paul's Hospital, Vancouver*

A Short Introduction to Understanding and Supporting Children with Eating Disorders

Lucy Watson and Bryan Lask

A Short Introduction to
Understanding and Supporting Children with Eating Disorders

Jessica Kingsley *Publishers*
London and Philadelphia

The illustrations in this book have been reproduced with permission from *Can I Tell You About Eating Disorders* (Lask and Watson, 2014).

First published in 2016
by Jessica Kingsley Publishers
73 Collier Street
London N1 9BE, UK
and
400 Market Street, Suite 400
Philadelphia, PA 19106, USA

www.jkp.com

Library of Congress Cataloging in Publication Data
Names: Watson, Lucy (Lucy Rebecca), 1991- author. | Lask, Bryan.
Title: A short introduction to understanding and supporting children with eating disorders / Lucy Watson and Bryan Lask.
Description: London ; Philadelphia : Jessica Kingsley Publishers, 2016. | Includes bibliographical references and index.
Identifiers: LCCN 2015044102 | ISBN 9781849056274 (alk. paper)
Subjects: LCSH: Eating disorders in children. | Eating disorders in children--Treatment. | Eating disorders in adolescence. | Eating disorders in adolescence--Treatment. | Anorexia nervosa.
Classification: LCC RJ506.E18 W38 2016 | DDC 616.85/2600835--dc23 LC record available at http://lccn.loc.gov/2015044102

British Library Cataloguing in Publication Data
A CIP catalogue record for this book is available from the British Library

ISBN 978 1 84905 627 4
eISBN 978 1 78450 102 0

Printed and bound in Great Britain

In memory of Professor Bryan Lask
18 February 1941–25 October 2015

DEDICATIONS

Lucy wishes to dedicate this book to her A Level Psychology teachers: Mr S Crumblehulme and Mr M Lynch, for it is what teachers are that is more important than what they teach.

Bryan wished to dedicate this book to his father's father, David Mordechai Lask, who, as a Head Teacher in Leeds in the 1930s and 1940s, inspired a generation of immigrant and refugee children.

ACKNOWLEDGEMENTS

We would like to acknowledge Pauline Jones and Gary Watson for their very helpful comments on an earlier draft, and all of those who have taught us so well.

CONTENTS

A SHORT INTRODUCTION

We decided to write this book because we believe there is a need for a short, accessible, easy-to-read volume on eating disorders for teachers and parents, who are exposed to these illnesses on a daily basis, often without knowing so. It is for those people who are usually battling hectic schedules and as such do not necessarily have the time to read comprehensive texts or scientific articles. In addition, we wished to write a book that dispelled common myths and misinformation about eating disorders.

In the first chapter we explain what eating disorders are, including case examples and illustrations to distinguish between different types of eating disorders. The second chapter uses a baking analogy to illustrate what is currently known about the causes of eating disorders. In the third chapter we focus on the features the reader should look out for in regards to whether or not a child or young person is suffering with an eating disorder. In the final chapter we concentrate on management.

Throughout the book we make reference to both genders, acknowledging that while certain disorders are more common to one gender, both genders can be affected.

As this is 'A Short Introduction', we also acknowledge that while there is a wide spectrum of eating disorders, we have chosen to focus on those we see most often in our clinical practice. We have, however, included some suggestions for further reading as required.

We hope that through furthering understanding of the underlying problems young people with eating disorders face, we can discourage stigmatising attitudes towards them, and we endeavour to propose ways in which they can be helped.

CHAPTER **1**

UNDERSTANDING EATING DISORDERS

WHAT IS AN EATING DISORDER?

In this book we use the term 'eating disorder' to refer to markedly disturbed eating behaviour. Sometimes such behaviour is accompanied by an abnormal, unhealthy and excessive preoccupation and dissatisfaction with body weight and shape, as is seen in anorexia nervosa and bulimia nervosa (see later in this chapter). However, the majority of children with disturbed eating do *not* have these body weight and shape concerns, yet they do have unusual or abnormal eating patterns for other reasons. Such eating patterns are not at all uncommon and include: restricted food intake, excessive food intake and marked fussiness around eating. It is the severity, rather than the nature, of such behaviours that determines whether or not they constitute a disorder that requires professional help.

It is also useful to remember that even without necessarily realising it, we all naturally avoid certain types of food. Most children, unsurprisingly, love sweet tastes (e.g. sweets, cakes and fruit juice) but are often put off by bitter or sour tastes (e.g. grapefruit, Brussels sprouts and coffee). Similarly, certain foods may be avoided because of their appearance, smell, colour or texture, or due to their association with an unpleasant memory. This does not necessarily mean the child has an eating disorder.

It is only if the eating behaviour is having an adverse effect upon the child's physical or emotional wellbeing that it should be a cause for concern. It is not uncommon for parents and other adults to be unduly concerned about a child's eating behaviour, and as such they may inadvertently create a problem through their own anxiety or by using coercion. On the other hand, parents, teachers or professionals may 'play down' the problematic eating, with equally adverse consequences.

Although eating disorders are extraordinarily hard to understand and potentially very problematic, if diagnosed early and treated correctly, full recovery can be expected in the majority. We therefore attempt to help the reader with early recognition and advice on how they can assist in ensuring the best possible outcome.

THE SPECIFIC EATING DISORDERS

It may be helpful to think of 'eating disorders' as an umbrella term that encompasses a wide range of differing problems (see Figure 1). Whilst each eating disorder has its own specific characteristics, there are also various similarities shared between them.

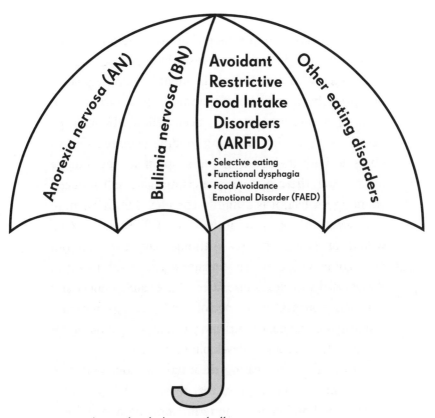

Figure 1: 'Eating disorders' as an umbrella term

We will now discuss each of the specific eating disorders in turn.

Anorexia nervosa (AN)

Anorexia nervosa is the most familiar, though *not* the most common of the eating disorders, perhaps due to its seemingly continuous media attention. Consequently, many myths and misunderstandings have arisen. For example, anorexia nervosa has been believed by many to be a lifestyle choice of young, middle-class females, so obsessed with their weight and shape that they indulge in extreme dieting, over-exercising and self-induced vomiting. In fact, it is a highly complex, life-threatening illness with a poor prognosis – not a 'lifestyle' anyone would or could choose. Although anorexia nervosa most commonly occurs in females aged 15–25 living in Westernised societies, it also affects males and younger and older age groups across a range of families in regards to race and religion, economic status and parental occupation, and is increasingly occurring in developing countries.

Just as the label 'eating disorder' has contributed to the common misperception that these disorders revolve around food and eating, the term 'anorexia nervosa' is a misnomer, as it literally means 'nervous loss of appetite'. It is particularly misleading, as those suffering with anorexia nervosa usually have good appetites, among a multitude of additional features that cannot be explained by loss of appetite or starvation.

Alice, aged 13, offers a good example. She used to be one of those girls who oozed happiness and positivity, a popular member of her class. Although somewhat of a perfectionist, spending hours on her homework, and perhaps with a slightly rigid, detailed approach to life, she was praised for her academic success and admired by her peers.

Like many other girls of her age, Alice liked reading popular magazines, often particularly focusing her attention on the health and beauty articles that dominated the pages. She also used numerous social media sites such as Facebook, Twitter and Instagram, which often promoted similar stories regarding celebrities' weight gain or weight loss and their strategies to do so.

After a talk on healthy eating at school, Alice had begun to think more about her own body and started to compare herself with the celebrities she was reading about and with photos of her peers posted on their own social media accounts. She became increasingly unhappy with her body and decided she needed to lose some weight and 'become healthier'.

Alice took up running and explained to her parents that she would be following a healthy eating programme she had found on the internet (not mentioning that this was actually a weight-loss programme for people who were clinically obese). Her parents were at first unconcerned, knowing that there had been a healthy-eating talk at school, and both were members of the local gym so didn't question Alice's decision to take up running after school.

Alice began to skip breakfast and became more insistent on what could be cooked for family meals and increasingly rigid over when and for how long she would run. Her parents became increasingly worried but when they spoke to her about their concerns, she lashed out, getting angry, shouting, 'Can't you see I'm fat? I'm disgusting!' Although her parents tried to reassure her, Alice simply became more upset exclaiming, 'You're lying – you just don't understand!'

Although her parents had hidden the weighing scales, Alice sought them out on numerous occasions every day. Her food intake continued to decrease and with an increase in the amount and length of time she would go running, her weight fell rapidly and consequently her periods stopped. She had gone from the girl who could make anyone smile to a withdrawn, sad, isolated girl who increasingly made negative comments about herself – protesting as soon as anyone tried to tell her otherwise. No matter what Alice's parents did or said, nothing worked. It was as if she was completely unaware of what everyone else could see; no matter what anyone told her, she truly believed she was fat, ugly and useless. With no other strategies or energy left, Alice's parents sought help from their family doctor.

Alice's story highlights the characteristic features of anorexia nervosa: an intense preoccupation with body weight and shape, a distorted view of her body and an increasingly negative opinion of herself, all leading to inadequate food intake.

Although she started with the same intention as many people who go on a diet, i.e. to lose weight, Alice's story clearly illustrates that anorexia nervosa is much more complex than simply following a weight-loss plan to drop a dress size. Those suffering with anorexia nervosa have a much more intense drive to lose weight, avoiding eating whenever they can, and they develop a detrimental ability to suppress feelings of hunger. As is natural, hunger cannot be ignored, and at times those suffering with anorexia nervosa may 'give in', yet feel immediately appalled with themselves for doing so. This often leads to an overpowering need to get rid of what has just been consumed; sufferers may induce vomiting, take laxatives or exercise excessively.

We will discuss anorexia nervosa in further detail in Chapter 3.

Bulimia nervosa (BN)

Although marginally less familiar than anorexia nervosa, bulimia nervosa is actually far more common. It is characterised by cycles of food restriction, followed by bingeing, then purging, then restriction again and so on.

Beth, aged 16, was a loud, outgoing, sociable girl with a sparkling and spontaneous personality, who had always been the life and soul of the party. She had been the first of her friendship group to have a boyfriend, the first to have sex (unprotected) and the first to try a cigarette, and she was the one to have the first and last drink. Although Beth's parents knew she was rather extrovert and that she attended many social events, they were unaware of the extent of Beth's impulsive and potentially dangerous behaviour.

One night, Beth's mother woke hearing a noise downstairs. She went to the kitchen to investigate and was alarmed to find Beth sitting with only the light from the open fridge illuminating the room. A large amount of food was spread across the kitchen table, including a half-eaten birthday cake bought for her father's birthday the following day. Panicked by her mother seeing the amount of empty food wrappers, plates, bowls and the half-eaten birthday cake on the table in front of her, Beth fled the kitchen while shouting a tirade of abuse at her mother.

Beth locked herself in the upstairs bathroom and was extremely distressed by her reflection in the mirror above the sink. She saw the tears rolling down her cheeks, felt the large amount of food in her stomach and was utterly disgusted with the fat, uncontrolled, chocolate-covered face staring back at her from the mirror. It was at that moment that Beth dropped to her knees in front of the toilet and made herself sick.

Outside the bathroom door, Beth's mother stood, confused at what she had just observed and alarmed by the sound of her daughter's crying and vomiting. She had no idea how long this had been going on, nor what to do about it. It was 3am and she felt utterly helpless.

After flushing the toilet and washing her hands and face, Beth felt better. She came out of the bathroom and nodded when her mother said they needed to talk. She could see how worried her mother was and accepted a hug before admitting that this cycle of losing control and eating a huge amount of food, only to make herself sick afterwards, had been going on for a while. Both sat crying, experiencing Beth's guilt, blame, shame and disgust. They both agreed that Beth needed help.

Beth's secret bingeing and purging, along with episodes of restriction, are characteristic of bulimia nervosa, and we will discuss it in detail in Chapter 3.

Avoidant Restrictive Food Intake Disorders (ARFID)

Just as the term 'eating disorders' is used as an umbrella encompassing a wide range of differing problems (see Figure 1), ARFID is also a blanket term that covers a collection of feeding and eating problems. However, the main difference between anorexia nervosa, bulimia nervosa and ARFID is that ARFID includes feeding and eating problems that are *not* driven by weight and shape concerns, but happen for other reasons, which we will explain.

Due to the relative breadth of feeding and eating difficulties covered by ARFID, we aim to highlight only three types – the most common – to illustrate the variety of problems: selective eating; functional dysphagia; and Food Avoidance Emotional Disorder (FAED).

Selective eating

While most children go through a phase of eating only a narrow range of foods, the majority 'grow out' of what appears to be their 'fussy eating'. However, there are some children who will not progress past this common developmental stage, thus causing considerable concern.

Sam, aged seven, would eat only chips, bananas, cream crackers, Marmite sandwiches and baked beans, and he would only drink water. He had eaten the same narrow range of foods for what seemed like forever to his family, and now was even particular about the specific brands of his preferred foods. While Sam's immediate family had adapted to his 'fussy eating', knowing which foods to buy and which brand to choose, members of his wider family repeatedly voiced their concerns about this. Sam's parents tried every way they could think of to introduce new foods but this was met by extreme anxiety from Sam, who often would also complain that he was going to be sick. In addition, while Sam's parents obviously had increasing concerns about his eating habits, they also recognised that despite them, he was developing normally, i.e. was not underweight, and apart from when new foods were served, Sam was a happy child who had a number of friends and was doing well both at home and school. They started to become increasingly anxious when he refused invitations to sleepovers and birthday parties and as holidays abroad approached. When they spoke to Sam about this, he explained that while he did want to go to all of these events, he was worried that his preferred food would not be available and he would be faced with new foods.

We will discuss selective eating in further detail in Chapter 3 and show how it differs from the other eating disorders, specifically in that sufferers will eat a very narrow range of foods, despite eating adequate amounts of food overall.

Functional dysphagia

Functional dysphagia literally means 'fear of swallowing in the absence of a physical abnormality'. While those suffering with anorexia nervosa have a significant fear of weight gain, people with functional dysphagia suffer from a significant fear of swallowing, or choking, causing them to avoid food – especially solid or lumpy types. As such, they avoid food, not due to concerns about their body weight or shape, but because they are terrified of choking, gagging or vomiting.

Francesca, aged nine, had always been a very sensitive child who picked up on people's emotions, changes in tone of voice or facial expressions and worried more than other children in her class. In spite of this, she had a close group of friends and was quietly confident, while achieving well academically. She ate well, was never a fussy child and was growing normally and developing as expected until she was around seven years old.

Francesca's grandmother had come round to their house, as usual, for Sunday lunch. She was extremely close to the family, especially Francesca, whom she picked up from school every day while her parents were at work. For this particular Sunday lunch Francesca's father had made roast chicken – Francesca's favourite. The family sat down to eat and were laughing at a joke that Francesca's father had just told, when all of a sudden they became aware that Francesca's grandmother was choking on a chicken bone. The situation quickly escalated as Francesca's grandmother became unable to breathe. Francesca was panic-stricken.

At what felt like hours later, Francesca's grandmother had stopped choking and drunk some water, and everything returned to normal. Francesca did not move. She simply stared at her plate and was afraid to eat anything on it, fearful that she too would choke like her beloved grandmother.

For a few days after this incident Francesca refused to eat a single thing. While the total food refusal did pass, Francesca refused any solid food and anything lumpy. While originally annoyed with Francesca's demands, her mother was so concerned that Francesca was not eating anything she gave in and started pureeing food and even sieved a glass of orange juice, as Francesca refused to drink it with the 'bits in'. This continued for two years.

It is normal for functional dysphagia to be initiated by a specific event such as described above. Other examples include experiencing or witnessing vomiting or undergoing unpleasant investigations such as those that involve a tube being passed into the stomach. It is important to note that even a seemingly minor incident can trigger functional dysphagia in those with a predisposed personality (see Chapter 2).

Functional dysphagia, like selective eating, usually occurs in the context of an anxious personality. We will discuss it in further detail in Chapter 3.

Food Avoidance Emotional Disorder (FAED)

Food Avoidance Emotional Disorder (FAED) has many features in common with anorexia nervosa, but it differs significantly in that the food avoidance has nothing to do with fears of weight gain.

Freddie, aged 12, had always been a highly anxious child compared with his peers. Recently he had become increasingly worried, unhappy and upset, but with no understandable cause. When asked why he wasn't eating, Freddie would simply state that he was 'too worried' or 'too sad' to eat. As such, his food intake continued to drop, and he was only eating a fifth of what he previously ate, with considerable weight loss.

As Freddie's story illustrates, while he showed some features of depression (e.g. low mood, sleep disturbance and being easily distressed) and characteristics of anorexia nervosa (e.g. weight loss and food avoidance), he did not meet the full criteria for either diagnosis. Freddie's presentation is typical of someone suffering with FAED. He was suffering with low mood and anxiety that was affecting his appetite. Freddie did not have any concerns regarding his weight or shape, but was becoming increasingly physically unwell, as he was steadily losing weight and was no longer growing at age-expected levels.

As with all the eating disorders illustrated previously, we will discuss FAED in further detail in Chapter 3.

Other eating disorders

There are a number of other eating disorders that have not been mentioned previously and will not be covered in further detail in this book, either in order to alleviate confusion between them (e.g. bulimia nervosa and binge eating disorder) or because of the rarity of the disorders and subsequent lack of current research on them (e.g. pica and rumination disorder). These include the following.

- Binge eating disorder (BED) – the engagement in frequent episodes of eating significantly larger amounts of food than most people will eat, in a short space of time (i.e. a binge). Individuals may eat much more rapidly than normal, eat until they are uncomfortably full, eat when they do not feel hungry and eat alone to hide their eating behaviour. In a similar way to young people suffering with bulimia nervosa, people with binge eating disorder will feel as if they have lost control over their eating and once the binge is complete they will feel extremely guilty and disgusted with themselves. However, unlike people with bulimia nervosa, people suffering with binge eating disorder do not engage in any compensatory behaviour, such as vomiting or excessive exercising, for their 'binges'. Consequently, they may well be overweight or obese, though it is not unusual for them to be of a normal weight either.

- Pica – the eating of substances/items that have no nutritional value, e.g. paint or dirt. This will usually occur in association with other severe mental health disorders often associated with an impairment of general functioning.

- Rumination disorder – frequent regurgitation of food that may be spat out re-chewed or re-swallowed. This behaviour is not due to a medical condition and reflects marked emotional disturbance.

CHAPTER SUMMARY

- We use the term 'eating disorder' to refer to markedly disturbed eating behaviour.

- It is important to remember that many children (and adults) will naturally avoid certain types of food and may have unusual eating patterns, but this does not mean they have an eating disorder.

- The severity, rather than the nature, of eating behaviours, determines whether or not they constitute a disorder that requires professional help.

- It is best to think of 'eating disorders' as an umbrella term that encompasses a wide range of different presentations including:
  » anorexia nervosa
  » bulimia nervosa
  » Avoidant Restrictive Food Intake Disorders (ARFID) e.g. selective eating, functional

dysphagia and Food Avoidance Emotional Disorder (FAED).

- Abnormal, unhealthy and excessive preoccupation and dissatisfaction with body weight and shape usually accompany the disturbed eating behaviour of those suffering with anorexia nervosa and bulimia nervosa.

- Eating disorders are extraordinarily hard to understand and are potentially very problematic. If diagnosed early and treated correctly, full recovery can be expected in the majority.

CHAPTER 2

CAUSES OF EATING DISORDERS

While there is a large field of information available on eating disorders, there is still some uncertainty about their causes. It is clear that there is no single cause and that a combination of factors is required for an eating disorder to develop. However, whilst much is known about the contents of this combination, there remain some missing links.

To try and clarify this, we use the analogy of baking a cake (see Figure 2). For this, we need:

- the ingredients

- an oven

- some decorating materials.

These are analogous to what are known as the three Ps:

- predisposing factors

- precipitating factors

- perpetuating factors.

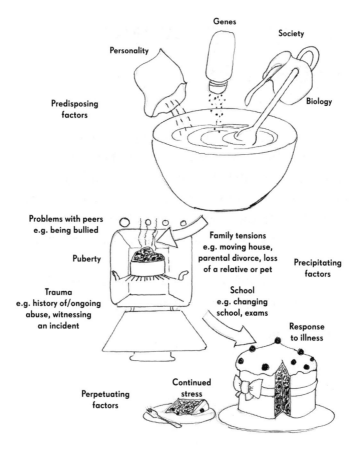

Figure 2: The development of an eating disorder

PREDISPOSING FACTORS (THE INGREDIENTS)

Like the ingredients needed to bake a cake, predisposing factors are necessary for a specific disorder to develop. For example, in many households flour, sugar, butter and eggs are naturally found in a cupboard or fridge. They may sit there for days or months on end, but they must be there to make a cake. Similarly, the predisposing factors are the basic items that already exist within any child or young person or in their environment. They do not make or trigger an eating disorder, but must exist for a disorder to emerge. Like the flour, sugar, butter and eggs needed to make a cake, there are various predisposing factors without which, no matter what the child or young person might experience, an eating disorder could not emerge. These are an individual's genes, biology and personality, and sociocultural factors.

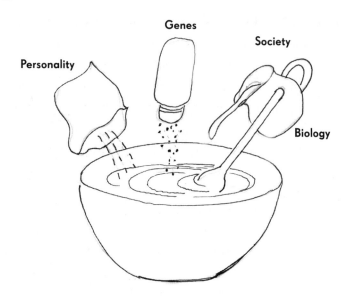

Genes

Only a minority of children suffering with eating disorders have close relatives who have previously had, or continue to suffer with, an eating disorder themselves. It might be surprising therefore that genes play any contribution to the development of eating disorders. Whilst it is extremely unlikely that one gene alone can contribute to the development of an eating disorder, genes are nonetheless essential ingredients. What we do know is that genes are a vital part of a number of other items that combine to create an eating disorder. This is just like how the flour needed to make a cake on its own would not create anything other than flour (and perhaps a messy kitchen) but blending it with other ingredients would give numerous possibilities.

Biology

While there is an ever-growing body of research into potential biological causes of eating disorders, for example abnormalities in brain chemistry, there is, as yet, no hard evidence for any specific biological factor. One of the key issues is how to differentiate between changes in the body that were present before the onset of the eating disorder, and may have influenced its development, and those that have occurred as a result of the eating disorder itself, such as changes due to the effects of starvation. For example, a young person suffering with anorexia nervosa will almost always be deficient in certain essential nutrients due to restricted food intake, but these nutritional deficits are a result of starvation and would not have caused the disorder.

While there is strong evidence of an abnormality in the body's chemical messenger system, the underlying process is not yet fully understood. Though there are many unanswered questions, and much more research is needed, emerging biological models have found abnormal activity in a part of the brain called the insula. As this abnormality does not appear to reverse with weight gain, it is likely to have preceded the illness and contributed to it. The insula can be likened to 'the central railway station of the brain' that contains many crucial routes passing through it (see Figure 3).

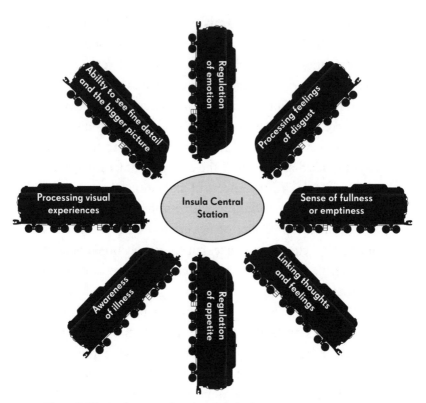

Figure 3: The insula – central station of the brain

Figure 3 illustrates the many routes, or 'train lines', that pass through the insula. Just like with any major train station, a fault will lead to problems and a fault within the insula will give rise to some, if not all, of the features of anorexia nervosa. For example, let's consider the train above called 'awareness of illness': when the route through the insula is working correctly, a child or young person would become aware if they were ill – and would thus usually tell their parents they were not feeling well.

However, if there were a fault on that line, or route, through the insula, the child might not be aware of being ill, just like those children or young people suffering with anorexia nervosa who genuinely do not realise how ill they are. There are many other examples that can be taken from Figure 3 suggesting that a fault within the insula plays an important part in the development of anorexia nervosa.

Personality

Personality characteristics can influence thoughts, feelings and behaviour. Different personality traits (e.g. confidence, patience, helpfulness, laziness, unfriendliness and self-centeredness) will affect attitudes, behaviour and outlook on life. Our individual personality style thus can affect how we feel about things, how we behave and how we think. Thus, certain types of personality can predispose to the development of an eating disorder as illustrated below.

Anorexia nervosa

As with Alice in Chapter 1, young people suffering with anorexia nervosa usually, but not always, present with hardworking, perfectionist and rigid personalities. They set themselves very high standards and will endeavour to achieve these, often in a seemingly obsessional, detail-focused way. For example, when set homework, young people suffering with anorexia nervosa may miss the bigger picture, tending to focus on minute details, meaning that though they may spend hours on a piece of homework, they do not have time to finish it. Due to the impeccably high standards that they set themselves, if they do not reach these standards they often experience feelings of failure and bouts of even lower self-esteem. The same rigid and perfectionist approach is seen in most other aspects of the young person's life. The impact of this approach can be hard to fully understand, as people suffering with anorexia nervosa are usually observed to be relatively quiet, compliant and obedient when compared with their peers. Additionally, there are rarely reports of problematic behaviour or concerns at school or home before the onset of the eating disorder, with many praising the young person for their conscientiousness.

Bulimia nervosa

Beth had a somewhat contrasting personality to Alice (see above and in Chapter 1). Those suffering with bulimia nervosa are often less compliant than those with anorexia nervosa and tend to be much more extrovert and defiant and have rather impulsive personalities. Due to their chaotic and impulsive personality types, people suffering with bulimia nervosa often participate in an array of risk-taking behaviours such as self-harm, alcohol and drug abuse and frequent, and often unprotected, sex.

In other words, confident, gregarious and impulsive personality types predispose an individual to develop bulimia nervosa rather than another disorder.

Avoidant Restrictive Food Intake Disorders (ARFID)

Children suffering with the other eating problems, such as those of Sam (selective eating), Francesca (functional dysphagia) and Freddie (FAED) described in Chapter 1, are predisposed to such eating difficulties, as they often have more anxious and sensitive personalities than their peers.

While the above are examples of personality traits that could predispose children or young people to certain eating disorders, that is not to say they apply to all those suffering with any specific eating disorder.

Sociocultural factors

Living in a society where food is readily available is an essential predisposing factor for anorexia nervosa and bulimia nervosa. In a society where food is readily available, being overweight may bring negative feedback. In contrast, in a society where food is limited, being on the larger side may bring positive comments, as it is an indicator of prosperity. In more affluent societies, therefore, thinness is idealised and over-valued and forms a path for individuals to follow, striving to gain the 'ideal' body shape.

It is well known that, especially in thriving Westernised countries, the media and fashion industry play a large role in maintaining pressure on individuals to achieve 'the perfect body', i.e. a thin one. The media, including social media, are inundated with the proposed ideal of thinness. Unfortunately, exposure to this bombardment of 'ideal' weights, shapes and appearances is now starting ever earlier in childhood. Growing up in a culture promoting dieting, exercising and dissatisfaction with the *normal* variation in weight, shape and appearance is problematic for any child, male or female. In the presence of other predisposing factors mentioned above, it is no wonder that such stresses could contribute to the development of anorexia nervosa or bulimia nervosa in either gender.

While the message to look after your body, your health and your standard of living is generally sensible, many public health campaigns are aimed at the adult population. One of the problems with advancing technology and children having access to smartphones earlier is that nothing is hidden from them. Even social media sites have adverts thrown on newsfeeds or down the sides of the website – many of which use our personal information to target which adverts are displayed. Unfortunately, for many youngsters this will mean they are exposed to dieting tips, advice, weight-loss programmes or products and a continued pressure to conform to the way many components of society depict we should be. It is clear, therefore, that, in combination with other predisposing factors, sociocultural factors predispose certain people to the development of an eating disorder.

PRECIPITATING FACTORS (ACCESS TO AN OVEN)

To return to the analogy of making a cake, once all the ingredients are placed in a bowl, stirred accordingly and poured into the appropriate cake tin, it is time to place them in the oven. As mentioned previously, without the basic ingredients an appropriate mixture could not have been made. Similarly, without the heat and time in the oven, the cake could not develop. The mixture is triggered to grow by the heat the oven offers and the time it is given, which are both needed to ensure the cake's progress.

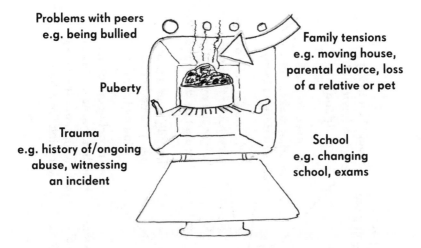

Problems with peers e.g. being bullied

Family tensions e.g. moving house, parental divorce, loss of a relative or pet

Puberty

Trauma e.g. history of/ongoing abuse, witnessing an incident

School e.g. changing school, exams

Just as the heat prompts (precipitates) the growth of a cake, specific precipitating factors trigger the development of a disorder. There are numerous examples of factors that could precipitate the onset of an eating disorder, and each individual will have their own individual stresses that precipitated the illness. It is important to be aware that there is no specific stress that can precipitate an eating disorder. We all vary, and what might be stressful for one person may not be for another, and vice versa.

However, one of the most common precipitating factors in the development of anorexia nervosa is the onset of puberty. Puberty is associated with a wide range of issues that can lead to undue stress or anxiety for the young person (see Figure 4).

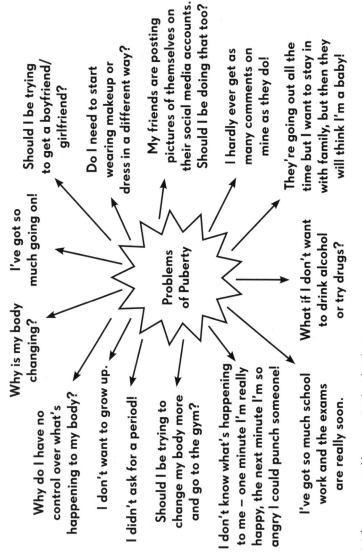

Figure 4: The common problems associated with puberty

As can be seen from the comments in Figure 4, children going through puberty become increasingly sensitive to their physical states and what is happening in their lives. While many are normal developmental changes, they can lead children to feel as though they are losing control of:

- their bodies (e.g. changes in their weight, shape and appearance and onset of menstruation)

- their social lives (e.g. peer pressure regarding physical appearance, social media involvement and engaging in other activities such as drinking, drugs or romantic relationships)

- their academic studies (e.g. feeling as though they are unable to continue with their academic success due to other pressures)

- their emotional state (e.g. feeling increasingly anxious about growing up and the behaviours and expectations associated with doing so).

Persistent feelings of losing control can lead some children to exercise control in other parts of their lives in an attempt to reclaim their identity and independence. For example, teenagers may change the way they dress or experiment with different hairstyles accompanied by trials of using make-up. They may also decide to radically redecorate their rooms or take up a new hobby – often sparking conflict with other family members. For example, one of the authors (LW) decided one day to change completely the entire layout of her room and in doing so broke her desk and, insisting that this was the desk's fault and not her own, demanded a replacement desk be bought the same day, much to her parents' frustration!

Many teenagers will go through a period of wishing to assert control, and this seems to be an essential part of adolescence in establishing personal style and future aspirations. However, some children going through these developmental changes will focus their need to regain control on their food intake. For example, they may see restricting the amount, or what, they eat as gaining control over one area of their life. To illustrate this, Figure 5 shows how assertion of control can have detrimental effects specifically in the development of anorexia nervosa.

Need for control: start restricting food intake.

Receive positive feedback on new healthy eating and exercise regime.

Lose weight. Hear or see on social media people commenting on how well they look, start sensing others' jealousy.

Feel good, have control: continue restricting food intake.

If lose control and eat: try harder to avoid eating, exercise more, lose weight and feel better.

Anorexia Nervosa

Figure 5: The downward spiral from needing control into developing an eating disorder

As mentioned previously, there are a number of precipitating factors that could trigger the start of an eating disorder. Each individual will have different stress thresholds and will thus react to certain events or situations in different ways. The example in Figure 5 is merely one of many stressors sufficient to precipitate anorexia nervosa. Other examples include: problems with peers, for example bullying, other traumas and specific problems at home or in school.

Puberty is a precipitating factor for the onset of bulimia nervosa, but not the other eating disorders, which tend to occur well before puberty. However, the main difference between those suffering with anorexia nervosa as opposed to bulimia nervosa is that when young people with bulimia nervosa become distressed, they tend to binge, followed by purging and then a period of restriction – sometimes known as the 'binge-purge-restrict cycle'.

ARFID usually occurs before the onset of puberty. Specific precipitating factors for these disorders may be difficult to establish and will commonly vary between individuals. The partial exception to the rule is functional dysphagia (fear of swallowing), which usually occurs after being involved in, or witnessing, a traumatic event such as the 'Granny choking' episode witnessed by Francesca (see Chapter 1).

Just as when baking a cake, with eating disorders it is quite difficult to do anything about the ingredients once they have been mixed. Nor is there much that can be done once the mixture is in the oven. However, once the cake is baked and taken out of the oven it is possible to change it considerably: adapting the shape or adding other layers, ingredients and decorations. Similarly, it is hard to do anything about the predisposing and precipitating factors in the development of an eating disorder, but the outcome can be influenced by those factors that maintain the disorder (perpetuating factors).

PERPETUATING FACTORS (SOME DECORATING MATERIALS)

We are now at the final stage of our cake analogy. We had the ingredients, which we stirred in our mixing bowl and placed in the oven. While in the oven the mixture was exposed to just the right amount of heat, time and shelf height. Now we have taken the cake out of the oven it is time to decorate it and wait for consumer feedback (e.g. in the case of an eating disorder, comments from others).

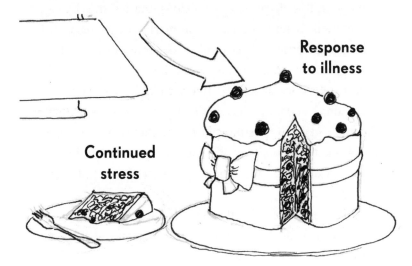

Just as when we switch off the oven but it stays hot for a while, which will affect the cake if we don't remove it, once an eating problem has developed, any precipitating factors that continue will affect and maintain the eating disorder. For example, if a child were bullied at school for being slightly overweight and then started dieting, that would form part of the array of precipitating factors. However, if the bullying continues after the onset of the eating disorder, it is likely to maintain the eating and/or associated behaviours.

There are often other factors that materialise following the onset of the eating disorder that can maintain the individual's behaviour(s). For example, if we think back to the downward spiral from needing control into developing an eating disorder (see Figure 5), a perpetuating factor for many people would be positive feedback. For example, when we make a cake and get positive feedback about how good it looks and how delicious it tastes, the chances are we will bake more cakes. Similarly, if a teenage girl who starts restricting her food intake constantly gets told how great she looks, or can sense others talking positively about her appearance, it is likely that she will continue restricting her eating, thus maintaining her eating disorder. As more girls are posting photos of themselves on their social media accounts, it is easier for them to get instant feedback on their appearance. This is another maintaining factor.

Many girls have social media accounts where they will post a new profile picture of themselves and wait to see how many 'likes' the picture receives. This not only fuels self-esteem, but also becomes a topic of conversation, or perhaps competition, with their peers. Many will now delete the picture they have uploaded within minutes if it has not received the self-required amount of 'likes'. It is this type of technology and social media use that can perpetuate the eating and associated behaviours of a person suffering with an eating disorder.

While self-esteem is usually already low, negative feedback can perpetuate the person's negative thoughts about themselves and serve to drive a continued need to have control over at least one part of their lives – their body shape.

Unfortunately, perpetuating factors may not be as clear-cut as the illustrations above. For example, if an individual has an undisclosed history of abuse, or is an on-going victim, if this experience is not identified it may understandably be maintaining the eating disorder. Similarly, if he or she is being bullied either at school, or online, and they have not disclosed this experience, it can be very difficult to understand their behaviour. Fortunately there is much that can be done to help (see Chapter 4).

In conclusion, there is no single factor that causes any eating disorder. It is the combination and interaction of many different factors that serve to create and maintain them. These are: the predisposing factors, i.e. the essential ingredients; the precipitating factors, i.e. those factors needed to trigger the emergence of an eating disorder; and the perpetuating factors, i.e. those that maintain the eating disorder. Just like our delicious cake, we had the ingredients, the right environment for it to be baked and the decorating materials to maintain and enhance its appearance (and our baking reputation).

CHAPTER SUMMARY

- Much is known about the causes of eating disorders but there are still many gaps.

- It is clear that there is no single cause and that a combination of factors is required for an eating disorder to develop.

- The predisposing factors – the basic items that already exist within any child or young person, or in their environment, that do not make or trigger a disorder but must exist for an eating disorder to develop – are:
  - » genes
  - » biology
  - » personality
  - » sociocultural factors.

- The precipitating factors – the features that trigger the development of a disorder – are:
  - » in anorexia nervosa and bulimia nervosa the most common precipitating factors include: puberty and any factor that is stressful to the child
  - » in Avoidant Restrictive Food Intake Disorders (ARFID) precipitating factors may be more difficult to establish and will commonly vary between individuals; functional dysphagia (fear of swallowing), usually occurs after being

involved in, or witnessing, someone choking or vomiting.

- Perpetuating factors – the features that maintain the eating disorder – are:

  » any triggering factors that persist, as these will affect and maintain the eating disorder, e.g. bullying, family stresses

  » other factors that often materialise following the onset of the eating disorder that can maintain the individual's behaviour(s) such as:

    • positive feedback, e.g. compliments, jealousy or envy of others

    • negative feedback, e.g. coercion.

CHAPTER **3**

WHAT TO LOOK FOR

With such an intense focus in Western society on 'healthy eating' and 'beautiful bodies', changes in children's eating habits can inadvertently lead to praise rather than concern. For example, if a child decides she is going to decrease the amount of 'fast food', 'fatty food' or 'snack food' she eats, with the explanation that they are 'unhealthy', many teachers, parents and carers alike would welcome this decision. Some children may also decide to stop eating red meat, or meat altogether, and again will produce explanations that may appear to sound like those they have heard during a 'healthy eating' talk. It is hard therefore to know when a change in eating behaviour is a cause for concern.

Similarly, it is not uncommon for children going through puberty to become sensitive to the changes in their bodies. An increased awareness of fashion and societal pressures to conform to the 'thin or muscular body ideal' are almost universal. However, at what point these typical adolescent interests cross into obsessions or bodily preoccupations can be difficult to ascertain, especially because of the secretive nature of anorexia nervosa and bulimia nervosa. In this chapter, we highlight the characteristics of each eating disorder and consider the similarities and differences between them. Rarely will all the features detailed be present in any one individual, and it is common to see much variation.

For simplicity, features to look out for have been categorised into four main areas:

- general features

- physical features

- psychological features

- food- and weight-related features.

We discuss how to manage these and other features specific to the eating disorders in Chapter 4.

ANOREXIA NERVOSA

The most common features of anorexia nervosa are summarised in Table 1. As mentioned previously, it would be unusual for all features to exist, with variation between individuals being not uncommon.

The tendency for children or young people suffering with anorexia nervosa to 'deny' or 'play down' any problems is very common. This is not lying, but an integral part of the illness, which reflects the brain dysfunction described in the previous chapter (see Figure 3). The affected child genuinely cannot experience how ill she is, and attempts at logic and reasoning by teachers, parents and carers, or other professionals, are doomed to fail. Indeed these attempts may actually aggravate the problem, as they intensify the sense of the young person's loneliness and/or isolation.

As Alice's story demonstrated in Chapter 1, anorexia nervosa is a seemingly illogical illness with those suffering from it truly believing that they are fat, ugly and useless. No matter what those around the sufferer say or do to state otherwise, no matter how ridiculous those beliefs may seem to others, the sufferer's stance cannot be easily changed.

As has been demonstrated previously, anorexia nervosa is an illness of misperception, misnomer, mystery and contradiction (see Table 1).

Table 1: The many contradictions of anorexia nervosa

Patient's thought/behaviour	Reality
'I feel fat.'	She is thin.
'I feel well.'	She is unwell.
'I feel full.'	Her stomach is empty.
'I have no control.'	She has considerable control over herself and those around her.
'I am a failure.'	She is very successful.
'I am useless.'	She is useful.
She is obsessed with food.	Yet she avoids it.
She starves herself.	But she may also binge.
She behaves with great strength.	She looks weak and fragile.
She sees many advantages to being thin.	She does not recognise the associated dangers.
She experiences the illness as a comfort and friend.	She is clearly tormented by it.
She was conscientious and compliant (before the illness).	She is defiant and rebellious (when ill).
She experiences our attempts to help as coercive (forceful and threatening).	She varies between resisting and accepting attempts to help.

Like Alice in Chapter 1, children and young people suffering with anorexia nervosa often have perfectionistic traits; they set themselves extremely high standards and work tremendously hard to achieve. As many of those suffering with anorexia nervosa are detail-focused and somewhat rigid in their approaches, they may repeat their work a number of times attempting 'perfection'. By being so detail-focused, those suffering with anorexia nervosa may miss the bigger picture. For example, when writing an English essay they may be so focused on every word being written in their best handwriting with no spelling mistakes that they end up writing the first paragraph five times. Consequently, they may not actually be able to complete the essay in time, or they may stay up extremely late to finish it. Praise for their hard work may reinforce the perfectionist approach.

In addition, anorexia nervosa is commonly associated with anxiety, depression, obsessive-compulsive behaviour and occasionally self-harm. Children suffering with anorexia nervosa can also exhibit restlessness, fidgetiness and over-activity, which are not conscious and determined but driven by over-activity within brain circuitry (see Chapter 2). Telling them to stop may work transiently, but it induces anxiety and resentment and the movements invariably return.

The common features of anorexia nervosa are listed in Table 2.

Table 2: Common features of anorexia nervosa

	Anorexia nervosa
General features	Onset usually between the ages of 12 and 18, but can be younger or older.
	More likely to affect girls than boys.
Physical features	Marked weight loss.
	Fatigue.
	Loss of menstruation or failure to start menstruating.
	Feeling full and getting stomach aches after eating only small amounts of food.
	Poor temperature control and low body temperature, subsequently feeling the cold more.
	Poor blood circulation, leading to general pale skin and cold hands and feet.
	Purple tinge to skin on hands and feet.
	Loss of any pubic or underarm hair; head hair may fall out.
	Lanugo (fine downy) hair on back and arms.
	Constipation.
	Physical lethargy or over-activity.
	Thin, fragile bones (detected by a special type of X-ray).

Table 2: Common features of anorexia nervosa (cont.)

	Anorexia nervosa (cont.)
	Low self-esteem.
	General lowering of mood.
	High levels of anxiety – not just around food.
	Obsessionality, perfectionism, secretiveness.
	Irritability.
	Low mood/depression.
Psychological features	Following rigid daily routines.
	Defiance/stubbornness.
	Wearing baggy clothes.
	Performing other self-harm activities (e.g. alcohol/drug abuse or scratching skin).
	Constantly commenting negatively about themselves, i.e. insisting they're fat when they're not.
	Withdrawing from social activity, even becoming socially isolated.
	Marked food avoidance with preference for very low-calorie foods.
	Denial of hunger.

	Hypersensitivity about eating.
	Preoccupation with food: spending long periods of time reading about food, cooking or preparing food for family meals.
	Self-induced vomiting.
	Increased intake of water/low-calorie fizzy drinks.
	Preference for eating alone, with an increase in other secretive behaviours.
	Leaving the table almost immediately after the meal, often going straight to the bathroom.
	Self-worth increasingly becoming associated with how much has been eaten/not eaten.
	Considerable anxiety, distress and irritability around meal times.
Food- and weight-related features	Particularly strange behaviour around food, e.g. cutting it into tiny pieces, moving it around the plate, smearing or crumbling it or hiding it to dispose of later.
	Increased use of salt, vinegar or spicy substances.
	Body-checking.
	Frequent weighing.
	Intense fear of weight gain.
	Use of laxatives/diuretics.
	Reading information on weight loss.
	Increased enthusiasm for activities involving exercise.
	Excessive exercising, particularly before or after eating.

BULIMIA NERVOSA

As mentioned in the introduction to this chapter, many of the eating disorders share a number of features. Anorexia nervosa and bulimia nervosa are prime examples, with much overlap between the two. Furthermore, it is not uncommon for children or young people suffering with either of these disorders to cross over to the other diagnostic category (e.g. from anorexia nervosa to bulimia nervosa or, less commonly, vice versa). As such, much of the following section on bulimia nervosa will already have been covered above. However, some specific features of bulimia nervosa are also summarised (see Table 3).

In Chapter 1, Beth's story highlighted the characteristic feature of bulimia nervosa: the 'binge-purge-restrict cycle' (see Figure 6). Unlike those with anorexia nervosa, people suffering with bulimia nervosa will often find they can't stop themselves from eating and will feel they have completely lost control. During such episodes of overeating, known as a 'binge', the child with bulimia nervosa will eat what the average person would deem as an excessive amount of food, i.e. many more times that of an average meal. The contents of a 'binge' will vary from person to person, as well as from one binge to the next. As those with bulimia nervosa share the same core body weight and shape concerns as children with anorexia nervosa, once they have 'binged' they feel deeply guilty, ashamed and disgusted with themselves for losing control. As they are also extremely self-critical and judge themselves by their appearance, young people with bulimia nervosa will often try and rid themselves of what they have just eaten by self-induced vomiting.

Occasionally, other means are employed to lose weight, including use of laxatives and/or diuretics, food restriction and excessive exercising. Due to weight fluctuations, some girls who have started their periods prior to the onset of bulimia nervosa may continue to have them but on an irregular basis, or their periods may stop completely.

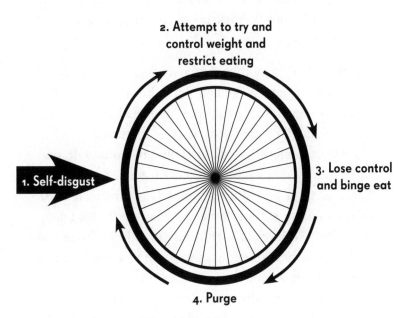

Figure 6: The Binge-Purge-Restrict Cycle

- **Step 1:** People suffering with bulimia nervosa have a preoccupation with weight and shape, which leads them to become highly self-critical to the point of self-disgust.

- **Step 2:** The self-disgust becomes the driving force to try and control weight.

- **Step 3:** Although people with bulimia nervosa may attempt to diet or limit or control their intake, they invariably lose control and binge as a form of self-comfort.

- **Step 4:** After the binge, there are intense feelings of guilt, shame and self-disgust and attempts are made to alleviate the distress by purging (self-induced vomiting).

People suffering with bulimia nervosa are usually so disgusted by their binge and purge behaviour that they will then attempt to try and control themselves once more by restricting their diet, and the cycle continues.

People suffering with bulimia nervosa will also often display a range of additional features such as self-harm, alcohol and drug abuse, having frequent and/or unprotected sex and other impulsive and risk-taking behaviour. Feelings of worthlessness, failure, shame and self-disgust, and subsequent low mood underlie these abnormal behaviours.

Although the disorder most commonly occurs in females who have gone through puberty, usually aged 14 and over, it can occur earlier and can also affect males. As is the case with anorexia nervosa, those suffering with bulimia nervosa have not chosen to be ill. They do not choose to overeat nor to feel so disgusted with themselves. They engage in serious, chaotic and dangerous behaviour, both through purging and partaking in other forms of risk-taking. The cause of such behaviour is mainly due to the young person's self-disgust. It is a harrowing experience for all involved and a very difficult disorder to understand, making it very hard for parents, carers and teachers to know how best to help and support those with bulimia nervosa.

In addition to the above, bulimia nervosa is commonly associated with depression and self-harm, which will also need treatment. In regards to self-harm, it is important to acknowledge that the young person is damaging or injuring their body as a way of dealing with or expressing overwhelming feelings and/or distress, which can also be a cry for help. Working with the young person to find alternative ways to express these feelings or alleviate unbearable suffering is paramount.

Table 3: Common features of bulimia nervosa

	Bulimia nervosa
General features	Affects girls far more than boys. Onset between aged 14 and 18, but can be earlier or later.
Physical features	Fluctuations in weight, though generally stay around an average weight. Occurrence of mouth ulcers and tooth erosion. Swollen cheeks due to swelling of the salivary (parotid) glands, a consequence of vomiting. Thickened skin on the back of fingers where they have continually been rubbed against the teeth as part of self-induced vomiting behaviour. Loss of or irregular menstruation or failure to start menstruating.
Psychological features	Low self-esteem. Difficulty sleeping. Increasingly defiant/stubborn. Performing other self-harm actions (e.g. alcohol/ drug abuse or scratching/cutting). Constantly commenting negatively about themselves, i.e. insisting they're fat when they're not. Mood variation. Excessive exercising, particularly before or after eating. Increased likelihood to make impulsive decisions such as getting piercings or tattoos.

Food- and weight-related features	Binge eating.
	Collecting and/or storing food.
	Sensitivity about eating.
	Self-induced vomiting.
	Increased intake of water/low-calorie fizzy drinks.
	Preference for eating alone, with an increase in other secretive behaviours.
	Leaving the table almost immediately after the meal, often going straight to the bathroom.
	Self-worth increasingly becoming associated with how much has been eaten/not eaten.
	Frequent weighing.
	Fear of weight gain.
	Use of laxatives/diuretics.

AVOIDANT RESTRICTIVE FOOD INTAKE DISORDERS (ARFID)

As indicated in Chapter 1, due to the range of eating difficulties that the blanket term ARFID covers, we have highlighted the three most common presentations: selective eating; functional dysphagia; and Food Avoidance Emotional Disorder (FAED).

Selective eating

The most common features of selective eating are summarised in Table 4.

More boys than girls experience selective eating and occasionally there may be a close relative who has had a history of similar problems. The term 'selective eating' is used to describe those who eat only a very narrow range of foods over a period of many years. Typically they eat about 10–12 different foods, usually high in carbohydrates, and often only specific brands, and some people may even be particular about from which shops the food is bought. When attempts are made to expand the range of food, the selective eater will become extremely distressed and cannot be coaxed into trying anything new, no matter what strategies are used. This aversion may be met with gagging or retching, although problems with swallowing their preferred foods are usually non-existent.

While 'fussy eating' is very common in toddlers, as children grow older if such eating habits persist they can dramatically affect a child's social functioning, leading to isolation both in and out of school. For example, if a child has a restricted diet, birthday parties, school trips, sleepovers or holidays abroad become increasingly problematic. Selective eaters are usually seen clinically between the ages of 7 and 11, after their parents become increasingly concerned about the social impact of their eating habits in addition to continued worry about their child's growth and nutritional development.

In relation to the latter, perhaps somewhat surprisingly, selective eaters tend to develop normally and are often the appropriate weight and height for their age. There are occasional exceptions to this rule, especially for those children who have particularly poor or restricted diets. Selective eaters differ from those suffering with anorexia nervosa and bulimia nervosa, as they do not share a concern with their body weight or shape, and are usually of a normal weight. Similarly, they do not have the problems experienced by those with other forms of ARFID such as a fear of swallowing or choking – unless perhaps a new food is introduced – nor do they show any anxiety regarding eating a normal amount of food, as long as it is in their preferred range. Thus, while their eating habits may affect their ability to socialise, most selective eaters do not generally present with many more problems than their normal peers.

However, some selective eaters may also have other problems, such as anxiety, determination to stick to certain routines, resistance to new experiences – for example wishing to wear the same clothes. New people, places or disruptions to the preferred or previously established routine may be particularly problematic for them, and making friends can be difficult. Although these types of behaviours are not uncommon in people with autistic spectrum disorders, only a minority of children with selective eating problems show the core phenomena of autistic spectrum disorders, i.e. difficulties with imagination and creativity, repetitive behaviours and hand/finger mannerisms or social and communication problems, such as a lack of integrated eye contact while talking.

As selective eaters enter adolescence, their repertoire of food often increases, perhaps due to peer-group and social pressure and the desire to participate in normal social activities. However a very few continue to eat selectively into adulthood.

Table 4: Common features of selective eating

	Selective eating
General features	Becomes evident as a problem around age six. Affects far more boys than girls. Usually resolves spontaneously during adolescence.
Physical features	Usually will be of a normal weight and height. Potential dental hygiene problems, especially if the selective range of food is high in sugar.
Psychological features	Anxiety around, or refusal to go on, school trips, sleepovers, parties etc. due to concern that their preferred foods are not going to be available. May display some obsessional behaviours, e.g. wishing to wear the same clothes or line up their school items on their desk and becoming distressed when a usual routine is disrupted.
Food- and weight-related features	Only eating a very narrow range of up to about 12 foods (thus will usually take a pre-packed lunch to school). Often demanding the same brand of food and that it is bought from a specific shop(s). Intense distress when confronted with 'new' foods. Noticeable anxiety and/or distress if confronted with an un-preferred or new food.

Functional dysphagia

The most common features of functional dysphagia are summarised in Table 5. The main distinguishing feature of such children is their fear of swallowing solid or lumpy foods.

Table 5: Common features of functional dysphagia

	Functional dysphagia
General features	Usually aged between 7 and 12. Affects boys and girls equally. Sudden onset with identifiable trigger.
Physical features	Depending on the length of time the individual has been suffering with functional dysphagia, they will present as rather short and thin in relation to their peers. However, if they have had a recent onset, they will be observed to lose weight rapidly.
Psychological features	Tendency to suffer with anxiety.
Food- and weight-related features	Noticeable anxiety and fear if presented with certain foods, complaining that they are going to choke or be sick. Avoiding eating and drinking solid or lumpy foods. May only eat pureed food or pre-made acceptable food for the individual, i.e. avoiding foods of a certain taste or texture.

Food Avoidance Emotional Disorder (FAED)

The most common features of FAED are summarised in Table 6.

As described in Chapter 1, FAED is often confused with anorexia nervosa and/or other mental health disorders such as anxiety or depression. The confusion arises because those suffering with FAED have lost, and continue to lose, weight as a consequence of avoiding food. However, people with FAED do not have the same intense body weight and shape concerns as those suffering with anorexia nervosa, nor do they have a distorted body image, i.e. thinking they are fat when they are thin. People with FAED avoid food because of intense anxiety and/or low mood. Whilst it is not at all unusual to lose one's appetite temporarily, for example because of anxiety or sadness around a specific event, the reduced food intake is temporary. In FAED, the food avoidance may last for many months or longer, is not related to a specific event and is associated with *continuous* feelings of worry/anxiety or sadness/low mood or a battle with obsessions that *persistently* interfere with their eating habits and overall appetite.

FAED affects children – both boys and girls equally – between the ages of around 5 to 16 years old. They present with emotional problems that lead to generalised sadness, anxiety and food avoidance, but there is no concern about body image. Although FAED is commonly associated with anxiety and depression, such children do not fulfil the criteria for a diagnosis of either of these.

Table 6: Common features of Food Avoidance Emotional Disorder (FAED)

	Food Avoidance Emotional Disorder (FAED)
General features	Usually between the ages of 5 and 16. Affects boys and girls equally.
Physical features	Will appear much slimmer than their peers.
Psychological features	Will explain they are too worried or sad to eat. Will show features of depression, e.g. low mood, looking tired (due to sleep disturbance) and frequently being upset. Will appear anxious and miserable, often having difficulty concentrating in the classroom. May display some obsessional behaviour, e.g. wishing to stay at home and avoid school. May avoid their peer group in the playground and the classroom.
Food- and weight-related features	Avoids food.

CHAPTER SUMMARY

- There is an intense focus in Western society on 'healthy eating' and 'beautiful bodies'.

- An increased awareness of fashion and societal pressures to conform to the 'thin or muscular body ideal' are almost universal.

- Changes in children's eating habits can inadvertently lead to praise rather than concern.

- There is great difficulty in ascertaining where and when changes in eating habits cross into obsessions or bodily preoccupations that should be a cause of concern.

- There are a number of features to look out for specific to different eating disorders clustered in four categories:
  » general features
  » physical features
  » psychological features
  » food- and weight-related features.

CHAPTER **4**

MANAGEMENT

We have now introduced the various childhood eating disorders (Chapter 1), provided information regarding their causes (Chapter 2) and detailed their clinical features (Chapter 3). In this chapter we: describe the essentials of management; advise about from whom to seek help; consider the role of school staff; and present some specific advice for the different eating disorders.

THE ESSENTIALS OF MANAGEMENT

There are various essential principles to understand and follow.

Eating disorders are complex and always need input from trained and skilled professionals

While it is essential not to lose sight of the healthy, positive side of the child or young person, it is crucial that this does not obstruct planning how best to help. For example, at times it may be difficult to differentiate between typical, age-appropriate behaviour and more concerning behaviours. The clearest example of this is when children enter puberty. They show enormous variation in behaviour, with mood swings, withdrawal, irritability, unpredictability and defiance, amongst many other previously uncharacteristic behaviours. Although this may be both worrying and frustrating, this is a normal developmental phase. However, it can be difficult to distinguish between the typical teenage behaviours described above and the more problematic behaviours associated with an eating disorder.

Throughout this process it is essential for adults to understand and accept that the child is unwell, is not choosing to be unwell and has a disorder that needs professional treatment.

Eating disorders are neither a voluntary behaviour nor a choice

Unfortunately, due to exposure to various false media portrayals around eating disorders, many laypeople and professionals alike believe much of the misinformation conveyed. No one chooses to have an eating disorder, which is in fact a torment to the child. Just telling them to eat more is as useless an instruction as telling someone with a chest infection not to cough. It is important to remember that the individual is still the same person as before becoming ill; they are being influenced by the illness. For example, when someone is ill they may be less sociable than usual and they may be more irritable, less empathic and so on. They were not always like that, and they will likely return to the way they used to be once the illness passes, but when they are *suffering* with the illness it will affect them in numerous ways – physically and psychologically.

The majority of people suffering with eating disorders appear attached, even dedicated, to their illness. This will be outwardly obvious by the defiant, stubborn behaviour that those around the person will often observe when they try and help. However, just as no one chooses to be ill, all would normally be desperate to be rid of the illness. Those with eating disorders behave differently, as if they are wedded to their disorder, often seeing advantages to the illness. Recognising, understanding, acknowledging and accepting this paradox is one of the keys to unlocking the enigma of eating disorders and anorexia nervosa in particular.

Believing that the child has chosen to have an eating disorder and could 'change' or eat 'if they put their mind to it' is not only incorrect but also likely to be a perpetuating factor, with chances of recovery being minimal. Indeed if that were the case, then eating disorders would be very easy to treat – just issue an instruction! Smokers may well be able to identify with this problem – if only all they had to do were to take advice and not smoke one more cigarette…if only it were that easy!

One of the most important points, therefore, is to try not to blame the child. Given the anxiety, distress and frustration that accompany attempts to help those with eating disorders, we fully acknowledge that avoiding blaming attitudes is difficult. It is normal to feel frustration and anger towards the child or young person. Trying to remember that it is the *eating disorder* that is instilling these feelings, not the child or young person themselves, is perhaps the most powerful tool in supporting them. In addition, it would be beneficial for all parties involved if expressions of frustration, helplessness or sadness for example, were reserved for situations away from the child suffering with the eating disorder. As the child will already be overwhelmed with such feelings as fear, self-disgust, guilt, shame and low self-esteem, hearing the outbursts of frustration by their parents, teachers or other carers, will only serve to plunge them further into self-loathing.

The reasons for developing an eating disorder are complex and not normally easy to understand, without deep and skilled exploration by a trained professional. Therefore such endeavours are best left to those with the appropriate training. However, there is much that parents, teachers and other carers can do to be helpful.

Although it is much easier in theory than in practice, acknowledgement and acceptance of the child's struggle is vital. The parents, teachers and other carers' expression of understanding and affection will go some way to negating the child or young person's feeling of worthlessness. Commonly, children with eating disorders describe themselves as 'a waste of space'. No matter how strong the resistance or withdrawal, it is important to remember that such behaviour is not chosen, and indeed actually leads the child to feel even worse about themself.

Parents and carers should always be informed of any concerns, be advised to seek professional help and be integral to management

Issues of confidentiality should *always* be trumped by the need to ensure the child's health and safety. Tragically, there have been instances of school staff (with the very best of intentions) counselling children without informing parents, only for the child to commit suicide.

No one individual, at home, school or within a clinic, should attempt to help or manage an eating disorder single-handed

As mentioned above, children suffering with eating disorders become controlled by and committed to their eating disorder. It is this attachment to the eating disorder that causes the child or young person to become resistant to change and extremely unwilling to accept help from others. Just as it is important to remember the young person has not chosen to have the eating disorder, their denial of a problem and subsequent resistance to seek or receive help are not just acts of defiance, rather an outward reflection of the fear within. For example, it is common to be terrified at the prospect of going to one's doctor, having found a lump somewhere in the body, given the possible implications. The fear of the unknown, or the thought of having to accept serious illness, could adversely influence help-seeking and acceptance.

In Chapter 2, we introduced the analogy of baking a cake, with the predisposing factors being the ingredients, the precipitating factors that ensured the growth of the cake being time and heat in the oven and the perpetuating factors being the adaptations to the cake once out of the oven, for example changing its shape and adding layers, additional ingredients and decorations. Whilst there is little that can be done regarding predisposing and precipitating factors per se, it can be helpful to be aware of such factors that may have triggered the development, or growth, of an eating disorder, as these may also serve as perpetuating factors, for example stress at home or bullying at school. What is most important is to try and ascertain the perpetuating factors, as these are most amenable to help.

It cannot be sufficiently emphasised that eating disorders are not just about eating or eating-related behaviours. For example, one of the core features in both anorexia nervosa and bulimia nervosa is low self-esteem. Although many parents, teachers and other carers focus on, and become increasingly worried about, the eating behaviour, the fundamental principle behind these behaviours is very low self-esteem. Young people suffering with anorexia nervosa and bulimia nervosa genuinely believe they are fat, ugly and gross; they have extremely low self-worth, feel disgusted with themselves, ashamed and guilty and often think they are failures both for eating (e.g. if they 'give in' to eating) and non-eating related behaviours (e.g. if they do not reach the high academic standards they have set for themselves).

For teachers, friends, siblings, parents and other people close to the child or young person, this can be particularly difficult to understand or deal with, especially when there appears to have been a dramatic shift in how they used to be. For those around the child or young person, hearing the negative views they hold for themselves and observing their obvious distress and self-disgust can be an upsetting experience. Trying to understand what it might be like to feel genuinely disgusted and ashamed with the way one looks, thinks or behaves is a powerful way of catching a glimpse of what is going on for the child and as such how best to help.

Unfortunately, both the feelings and subsequent eating disorder do not disappear overnight, or even over a month, and may well last for much longer. The carers, be they parents, nurses or teachers, are therefore also 'in it for the long haul'. While precipitating and perpetuating factors may well have been identified, there are no shortcuts to free the child of these, and helping them overcome these factors will be a lengthy process

FROM WHOM TO SEEK HELP

If an eating disorder is suspected by anyone in contact with the child, the parents should be informed at the earliest opportunity. The greater the delay in diagnosis and treatment, the poorer the outcome will be. It is completely understandable that sometimes other may be reticent about raising their concerns with the child's parents.. However, the serious nature of eating disorders, the potential for major physical and psychological complications and the fact that parents have responsibility for their child's wellbeing and must be central to management means that their need to know should always trump confidentiality concerns. Should the reader be in any doubt about this it is worth considering what would happen were a child to have a seizure or an asthma attack whilst in school but pleaded that her parents not be told. There would be no question about whether to inform them. The same indisputably applies to eating disorders. They are complex and often dangerous illnesses, rarely resolving without skilled attention, and often having a poor outcome. As the child with an eating disorder lives with her parents and eats most of their meals with them, it is *vital* that parents are fully aware of any concerns.

Should the parents ask from whom they should seek help, they should be advised to see their general practitioner at the earliest opportunity. In addition, recommending eating disorder charities such as Beat will also be useful for parents wishing to gain further advice about how best to proceed in regards to getting professional support (see Useful Organisations). Once parents have seen their local doctor, a referral may be made to the local Child and Adolescent Mental Health Service (CAMHS). These services will usually include a variety of multidisciplinary professionals including psychiatrists, psychologists, family therapists and dieticians who will be able to offer further, specialist advice to parents, teachers, and other professionals in contact with the child. Note that while some families may seek private assessment, it is worth emphasising that a multidisciplinary approach will offer the full package of care for the child or young person. For example, while dieticians can advise about dietary content, they cannot offer all the other necessary components of treatment.

ROLE OF SCHOOL STAFF

Notwithstanding these provisos there is much that school staff can do to help once they have informed the parents. When sharing their concerns with parents, school staff should also advise them about the importance of seeking professional help, usually from their local doctor.

Once professional help has been sought, a meeting between school staff and the child's parents is important. It is vital that all carers are consistent between each other and over time in their attempts to help. This applies particularly to parents, whether they are together or separated. Several decisions will need to be made, including deciding whether the child is well enough to be at school, if so whether to have meals at school, as opposed to home, and if at school, what level of supervision would be required. Decisions also need to be made about how much schoolwork and homework should be allowed.

Ultimately, just as in any team sport a group of athletes need to work in harmony, any team around an individual suffering with an eating disorder must work as one. Parents are the driving force in discussing and agreeing the approach they wish for themselves and others to take – hence the need for teachers to report any concerns regarding a change in a child's behaviour. Good teamwork is an essential component of managing an eating disorder.

SPECIFIC ADVICE FOR EACH EATING DISORDER

In the previous section we focused on the essential guidelines that are imperative when attempting to help people suffering with eating disorders. While we acknowledge that much of this next section has been mentioned previously, we now focus on pieces of specific advice required in order to help children and young people suffering with particular eating disorders.

Anorexia nervosa

- Parents are to be told as soon as concerns about a young person's behaviour (eating and otherwise) arise.

- Professional help should be sought as soon as possible.

- No action should be taken in regards to a young person's eating behaviour without full discussion with their parents.

- The need for consistency between contexts is paramount. For example, the same professional advice and management of meals should be followed both at home and at school.

- The young person's meal content and quantity should be advised by the young person's parents or by a dietician who is in liaison with them.

- Decisions need to be made in liaison with the parents regarding school meals, for example, whether the young person will bring a packed lunch to school or will eat at home.

- Consideration needs to be given around whether the young person is well enough to be at school and, if so, whether they are able to eat unsupervised.

- If the young person is having meals at school, it is preferable for them to have a separate dining area, eating under supervision.

- It is important not to cajole or pressurise the young person, nor to ask questions about why they find it hard to eat. The meal table is the last place to do this and it should not be done at school at all. A sympathetic acknowledgement is fine.

- Do not discuss weight and shape with the young person.

- Do not weigh the young person – this should only be done by the health professionals working with the young person.

- Although counterintuitive, do not praise or encourage the young person during meals – this will only serve to reinforce their feelings of shame and guilt.

- It is important that bathroom visits are not allowed for at least one hour after meals.

Bulimia nervosa

- Parents are to be told as soon as concerns about a young person's behaviour (eating and otherwise) arise.

- Professional help should be sought as soon as possible.

- No action should be taken in regards to a young person's eating behaviour without full discussion with their parents.

- The need for consistency between contexts is paramount. For example, the same professional advice and management of meals should be followed both at home and at school.

- The young person's meal content and quantity should be advised by the young person's parents or by a dietician who is in liaison with them.

- Decisions need to be made in liaison with the parents regarding school meals, for example, whether the young person will bring a packed lunch to school or will eat at home.

- Consideration needs to be made around whether the young person is well enough to be at school and, if so, whether they are able to eat unsupervised.

- If the young person is having meals at school, it is preferable for them to have a separate dining area, eating under supervision.

- It is important not to cajole or pressurise the young person, nor to ask questions about their illness. A sympathetic acknowledgement is fine.

- Do not discuss weight and shape with the young person.

- Do not weigh the young person – this should only be done by the health professionals working with the young person.

- Although counterintuitive, do not praise or encourage the young person during meals – this will only serve to reinforce their feelings of shame and guilt.

- It is important that bathroom visits are not allowed for at least one hour after meals.

- Snacking is to be dissuaded.

Selective eating

- Parents are to be told as soon as concerns about a young person's behaviour (eating and otherwise) arise.

- Professional help should be sought as soon as possible.

- No action should be taken in regards to a young person's eating behaviour without full discussion with their parents.

- The need for consistency between contexts is paramount. For example, the same professional advice and management of meals should be followed both at home and at school.

- The child's meal content and quantity should be advised by the child's parents or by a dietician who is in liaison with them.

- It is important not to cajole or pressurise the child, nor ask questions they would struggle to answer. A sympathetic acknowledgement is fine.

- Do not weigh the young person – this should only be done by the health professionals working with the young person.

- Favoured foods are to be encouraged.

- Bathroom visits after meals are okay.

Functional dysphagia

- Parents are to be told as soon as concerns about a young person's behaviour (eating and otherwise) arise.

- Professional help should be sought as soon as possible.

- No action should be taken in regards to a young person's eating behaviour without full discussion with their parents.

- The need for consistency between contexts is paramount. For example, the same professional advice and management of meals should be followed both at home and at school.

- The child's meal content and quantity should be advised by the child's parents or by a dietician who is in liaison with them.

- It is important not to cajole or pressurise the child, nor ask questions about their problem with eating. A sympathetic acknowledgement is fine.

- Do not weigh the young person – this should only be done by the health professionals working with the young person.

- Favoured foods are to be encouraged.

- Pureed, soft and similar foods are also to be allowed.

- Bathroom visits after meals are okay.

Food Avoidance Emotional Disorder (FAED)

- Parents are to be told as soon as concerns about a young person's behaviour (eating and otherwise) arise.

- Professional help should be sought as soon as possible.

- No action should be taken in regards to a young person's eating behaviour without full discussion with their parents.

- The need for consistency between contexts is paramount. For example, the same professional advice and management of meals should be followed both at home and at school.

- The child's meal content and quantity is to be advised by the child's parents or by a dietician who is in liaison with them.

- Decisions need to be made in liaison with the parents regarding school meals, for example, whether the child will bring a packed lunch to school or will eat at home.

- Consideration needs to be made around whether the child is well enough to be at school and, if so, whether they are able to eat unsupervised.

- If the child is having meals at school, it is preferable for the child to have a separate dining area, eating under supervision.

- It is important not to cajole or pressurise the child nor ask questions about their illness. A sympathetic acknowledgement is fine.

- Do not discuss weight and shape with the child.

- Do not weigh the young person – this should only be done by the health professionals working with the young person.

- For some it may be beneficial to praise or encourage the child during meals, however do ask for advice from parents before doing so, as they will have consulted with professionals.

- Bathroom visits after meals are okay.

While these are specific suggestions in order to help children and young people suffering with an eating disorder, it cannot be stressed enough that professional help and support should be sought as soon as any concerns arise about a child's eating behaviour or changes in behaviour or emotional state are noted.

There are many similarities and differences across the different eating disorders and as such their treatment will also have similarities and differences. It is thus essential to know the right diagnosis to ensure the child or young person suffering with a particular eating disorder gets the appropriate treatment – and this can only be done if professional help is sought.

CHAPTER SUMMARY

- There are a number of essential principles that are crucial to follow in regards to the management of eating disorders.

- It is imperative that professional help is sought.

- School staff members play a vital role in conjunction with parents/carers and professionals trained in eating disorders.

- While similarities between them do exist, different eating disorders need to be managed in specific ways.

A SHORT CONCLUSION

We have aimed to provide short, accessible, easy-to-read information on eating disorders for parents, carers, teaching staff and other professionals working with children. Throughout, we have described the different types of eating disorders, current knowledge regarding what causes them, what to look out for and ways to manage them. We hope that through reading each chapter the reader has been able to collect vital pieces of information that have contributed to a clearer picture of eating disorders themselves and what individuals struggle with.

While we acknowledge readers may not have any time to gain a deeper understanding through further reading, for those who do, we include a recommended reading list at the end of this book, including resources to be read by, or with, children. *Can I tell you about Eating Disorders?* in particular uses the same case names, illustrations and analogies as this book to explain simpler versions of information for classroom-age children. Therefore, the two books can be used in tandem to aid both adult and child understanding of such complex conditions.

We would also emphasise the importance of thinking not just about the child or young person and their needs, but also the stress felt by the child's parents and carers, siblings, teaching staff and other professionals involved in the child's care. As part of the wider system surrounding the child, teachers and parents have a vital role in contributing to help the child, their family and friends to help get rid of the eating disorder causing so much physical and emotional pain. As part of this, teachers and parents can educate their peers, friends, family and colleagues about eating disorders. Through this book our aim has been to dispel myths, aid understanding, challenge misperception and misunderstanding and assist the reader to do the same. Through gaining a clearer idea of the puzzling nature of eating disorders, teachers and parents can aid others in resolving their mystery too.

ABOUT THE AUTHORS

Lucy Watson is an Assistant Psychologist at the Michael Rutter Centre, Maudsley Hospital. She has co-authored the children's book, *Can I tell you about Eating Disorders?* and is the Editorial Assistant for the journal *Advances in Eating Disorders: Theory, Research and Practice*, edited by Dr Rachel Bryant-Waugh.

Bryan Lask was Emeritus Professor of Child and Adolescent Psychiatry at St George's, University of London, UK, Visiting Professor at the University of Exeter, Medical Director at Rhodes Farm Clinic, London and Honorary Consultant Psychiatrist at Great Ormond Street Hospital.

RECOMMENDED READING

FOR YOUNGER READERS OR THOSE WHO WISH TO TALK TO CHILDREN ABOUT EATING DISORDERS

Lask, B. and Watson, L. (2014) *Can I tell you about Eating Disorders?* London: Jessica Kingsley Publishers.

FOR PARENTS WHO WISH TO GAIN MORE INFORMATION

Bryant-Waugh, R. and Lask, B. (2013) *Eating Disorders: A Parents Guide (2nd edition).* East Sussex: Routledge.

FOR PROFESSIONALS WHO WISH TO TACKLE A MORE COMPREHENSIVE TEXTBOOK

Lask, B. and Bryant-Waugh, R. (2013) *Eating Disorders in Childhood and Adolescence (4th edition).* East Sussex: Routledge.

USEFUL ORGANISATIONS

Beat – beating eating disorders

Wensum House

103 Prince of Wales Road

Norwich

Norfolk

NR1 1DW

Email: info@b-eat.co.uk

Website: www.b-eat.co.uk

Beat is the UK's leading charity supporting individuals suffering with eating disorders and campaigning on their behalf.

F.E.A.S.T. (Families Empowered and Supporting Treatment of Eating Disorders)

PO Box 11608

Milwaukee, Wisconsin 53211

USA

Email: info@feast-ed.org

Website: http://members.feast-ed.org

F.E.A.S.T. is an international organisation supporting patients, families and clinicians working together to treat eating disorders.

National Eating Disorders Association (NEDA)

165 West 46th Street
Suite 402
New York, NY 10036
USA
Email: info@nationaleatingdisorders.org
Website: www.nationaleatingdisorders.org

NEDA is the leading non-profit organisation in the United States that advocates on behalf of and supports individuals and families affected by eating disorders.

YoungMinds

Suite 11
Baden Place
Crosby Row
London
SE1 1YW
Email: ymenquiries@youngminds.org.uk
Website: www.youngminds.org.uk

YoungMinds is the UK's leading charity committed to improving the emotional wellbeing and mental health of children and young people. Driven by their experiences we campaign, research and influence policy and practice.

INDEX